The TRIO Programs

Cassandria Dortch
Analyst in Education Policy

September 10, 2012

Congressional Research Service
7-5700
www.crs.gov
R42724

CRS Report for Congress
Prepared for Members and Committees of Congress

Summary

This report serves as an introduction to the TRIO programs. The TRIO programs are the primary federal programs providing support services to disadvantaged students to promote achievement in postsecondary education. This report provides a description of the TRIO programs, authorized in Title IV-A-2-1 of the Higher Education Act (HEA), as amended by the Higher Education Opportunity Act (HEOA; P.L. 110-315) in 2008. Key program amendments of the HEOA as implemented through final Department of Education (ED) regulations published in 2010 are discussed. The report is intended to support congressional understanding of the programs, summarize recent evaluations and performance reports, and review the Department of Education's progress in implementing HEOA.

In FY2012, the TRIO programs were funded at $840 million and served almost 800,000 secondary, postsecondary, and adult students. The TRIO programs have been designed to prepare qualified individuals from disadvantaged backgrounds for postsecondary education and encourage their success throughout the educational pipeline from secondary school to undergraduate and graduate education. While the TRIO programs primarily serve low-income, first-generation college students, they also serve students with disabilities, veterans, homeless youth, foster youth, and individuals underrepresented in graduate education. The TRIO programs are also designed to award prior grantees that implement successful projects and propose high-quality projects with subsequent grants before awarding applicants without prior TRIO experience.

There are six TRIO programs, each serving a different demographic. The TRIO Upward Bound (UB) Program serves secondary school students, providing relatively intensive preparation services and encouragement to help students pursue education beyond secondary school. the TRIO Talent Search (TS) Program provides less intensive services than UB in support of the completion of high school and enrollment in postsecondary education, and it encourages primarily students and out-of-school youth. The TRIO Educational Opportunity Centers (EOC) Program primarily serves adults. The TRIO Student Support Services (SSS) Program motivates undergraduate students to complete their undergraduate education. The Ronald E. McNair Postbaccalaureate Achievement (McNair) Program prepares undergraduate students for graduate school. Finally, the TRIO Staff Development (Training) Program trains TRIO project staff to be more effective.

Several TRIO program provisions were amended through the HEOA. Two key HEOA amendments address issues pertaining to the application review process: scoring and second reviews (appeals). The first amendment defined outcome criteria that require the secretary and each grantee to agree upon objectives/targets for the criteria. The extent to which grantees meet or exceed these objectives determines the number of prior experience (PE) points the grantee may earn as part of its application in the next grant competition. Earning more PE points increases the likelihood of funding. The FY2011 TS and EOC and FY2012 UB grant competitions requested that applicants propose objectives for the statutorily defined outcome criteria. The second amendment established an application review process by which those unsuccessful applicants that can identify a specific technical, administrative, or scoring error may have their applications reviewed a second time (appealed). The FY2012 TRIO UB competition is the first to use the revised application review process.

Contents

Background 1
Pipeline of TRIO Programs 2
  TRIO Upward Bound (UB) Program 2
    Eligible Recipients 2
    Program Participants 3
    Program Intensity and Activities 3
    Outcome Criteria 4
  TRIO Talent Search (TS) Program 5
    Eligible Recipients 6
    Program Participants 6
    Program Intensity and Activities 6
    Outcome Criteria 7
  TRIO Educational Opportunity Centers (EOC) Program 7
    Eligible Recipients 7
    Program Participants 7
    Program Intensity and Activities 7
    Outcome Criteria 8
  TRIO Student Support Services (SSS) Program 8
    Eligible Recipients 9
    Program Participants 9
    Program Intensity and Activities 9
    Outcome Criteria 10
  Ronald E. McNair Postbaccalaureate Achievement (McNair) Program 11
    Eligible Recipients 11
    Program Participants 11
    Program Intensity and Activities 11
    Outcome Criteria 11
  TRIO Staff Development (Training) Program 12
    Eligible Recipients 12
    Program Participants 12
    Program Intensity and Activities 12
    Outcome Criteria 12
  Comparison of Key Features of the TRIO Programs 13
Program Appropriations and Project Participants 15
Major HEOA Amendments to Common TRIO Provisions 17
  Required Program Activities 17
  Prior Experience Points 18
  Application Review Process (Appeal) 20
  Award Amounts and Numbers of Program Participants 21
  Length of Grant Award 21
  Multiple Grants for Different Populations 21
Research, Evaluation, and Assessments 22
  SSS Independent Evaluations 23
  SSS PART Reviews and Annual Performance Report Data 24
  UB Independent Evaluations 25
  UB PART Review and Annual Performance Report Data 27

TS Evaluations.. 28
TS PART Review and Annual Performance Report Data.. 28
EOC Evaluations 29
EOC PART Review and Annual Performance Report Data 29
McNair Independent Evaluations 30
McNair PART Review and Annual Performance Report Data 30
Training Evaluations.. 30

Tables

Table 1. TRIO Program Eligible Grant Recipients 13

Table 2. Comparison of the Required Program Participant Demographics across the TRIO Programs 13

Table 3. Comparison of the Required Program Activities for the Student Serving TRIO Programs 14

Table 4. TRIO Appropriations and Program Allocations: FY2006-FY2012 16

Table 5. Number of TRIO Participants: FY2008-FY2011 17

Table 6. Statutory Outcome Criteria for the Student-Serving TRIO Programs 19

Contacts

Author Contact Information... 30

Background

Since its inception, the Higher Education Act (HEA) of 1965 has had a focus on increasing the postsecondary access and achievement of disadvantaged students, including low-income and first-generation college students. The two major approaches are financial support or supportive services. The Pell Grant program is the single largest source of federal grant *aid* supporting primarily low-income postsecondary education students.[1] The Pell Grant program provided almost $33.4 billion to approximately 9.7 million undergraduate students in award year 2011-2012. The TRIO programs are the primary federal programs providing *support services* to disadvantaged students to promote achievement in postsecondary education.[2] The TRIO programs were so named by the 1968 HEA amendments, which consolidated a trio of programs that support the educational achievement of disadvantaged students under one title. The number of TRIO programs has since expanded to six, and they were funded a total of $840 million in FY2012.

Collectively, the TRIO programs are designed to identify qualified individuals from disadvantaged backgrounds, prepare them for a program of postsecondary education, provide support services for postsecondary students, motivate and prepare students for doctoral programs, and train individuals serving or preparing for service in the TRIO programs. TRIO services support the federal policy goals of secondary school completion, college preparation, college enrollment, undergraduate completion, and graduate school preparation. There are six main TRIO programs (in descending order of funding levels):

- TRIO Student Support Services (SSS) Program,
- TRIO Upward Bound (UB) Program,
- TRIO Talent Search (TS) Program,
- TRIO Educational Opportunity Centers (EOC) Program,
- Ronald E. McNair Postbaccalaureate Achievement (McNair) Program, and
- TRIO Staff Development (Training) Program.

The Higher Education Opportunity Act (HEOA; P.L. 110-315) of 2008 made several changes to the TRIO programs to increase accountability, rigor, and uniformity and to ensure that all disadvantaged students had access to the programs. In October 2010, the U.S. Department of Education (ED) released the final regulations to implement the HEOA TRIO program provisions.[3]

This report serves as an introduction to the TRIO programs. The initial section describes the provisions of each of the programs, as reauthorized by HEOA. The subsequent section provides a brief overview of recent funding and participation trends for each of the programs. This is followed by a description of unique provisions and regulations that are common to the TRIO

---

[1] For more information on Pell Grants, see CRS Report R42446, *Federal Pell Grant Program of the Higher Education Act: How the Program Works, Recent Legislative Changes, and Current Issues*, by Shannon M. Mahan.

[2] HEA Title IV-A-2-1; 20 U.S.C. §1070a-11 et seq.

[3] Office of Postsecondary Education and Office of Elementary and Secondary Education, Department of Education., "High School Equivalency Program and College Assistance Migrant Program, The Federal TRIO Programs, and Gaining Early Awareness and Readiness for Undergraduate Program," 75 *Federal Register* 65712-65803, October 26, 2010.

programs, highlighting key HEOA and regulatory changes. A concluding section presents the key findings and results of recent program evaluations and assessments.

Pipeline of TRIO Programs

The federal TRIO programs provide support services and some financial assistance primarily to low-income, first-generation college students to help them succeed academically and encourage them to advance through much of the educational pipeline. The TRIO programs work together to provide a pipeline of support services from secondary school through undergraduate and graduate education. Each of the TRIO programs is designed to serve a different target population of participants through a different level of education. The following subsections describe the purpose, eligible recipients, program participants, program intensity and activities, and outcome criteria of each of the TRIO programs and are ordered according to their sequence in the educational pipeline:

- UB primarily supports the college preparation of secondary students,
- TS primarily supports the postsecondary enrollment of secondary students,
- EOC primarily supports the postsecondary enrollment of adult students,
- SSS primarily supports the completion of undergraduate education,
- McNair primarily supports graduate school preparation, and
- Training supports TRIO staff development.

For a comparison of eligible grant recipients, program participant requirements, and required program activities, see **Table 1**, **Table 2**, and **Table 3**, respectively.

TRIO Upward Bound (UB) Program[4]

The UB program is intended to provide intensive preparation and encouragement toward success in education beyond secondary school. UB has three types of projects: Regular UB to prepare secondary school students for programs of postsecondary education, UB Math and Science Centers (UBMS) to prepare high school students for postsecondary education programs that lead to careers in the fields of math and science, and Veterans UB (VUB) to assist military veterans to prepare for a program of postsecondary education. Compared to Regular UB projects, UBMS projects typically serve more students in their junior or senior years, serve students with stronger math and science skills, and emphasize the summer component more.

Eligible Recipients

Grants or contracts are available to institutions of higher education (IHEs); public and private agencies and organizations, including community-based organizations (CBOs) with experience in

---

[4] HEA section 402C; 20 U.S.C. §1070a-13; 34 C.F.R. 645.

serving disadvantaged youth;[5] secondary schools;[6] and combinations of such institutions, agencies, and organizations.

Program Participants

All participants must have completed eight years of elementary education or be at least 13 years of age but not more than 19 years of age, unless the age and grade limitation defeats the purpose of the program. In addition, all participants must be in need of academic support to pursue education beyond secondary school successfully. At least two-thirds of the program participants must be low-income, first-generation college students. The remaining one-third of Regular UB and VUB participants must be low-income, first-generation, or at-risk of academic failure.[7] The remaining one-third of UBMS participants must be low-income or first-generation. The program defines a Regular UB participant who has a high risk for academic failure as an individual who is not at the proficient level on state assessments in reading or language arts; is not at the proficient level on state assessments in math; has not successfully completed pre-algebra or algebra by the beginning of the 10th grade; or has a grade point average of 2.5 or less (on a 4.0 scale) for the most recent school year. The program defines a military veteran who has a high risk for academic failure as an individual who has been out of high school or dropped out of a program of postsecondary education for five or more years; has scored on standardized tests below the level that demonstrates a likelihood of success in a program of postsecondary education; or meets the definition of an individual with a disability.

Program Intensity and Activities

Historically, UB has been a relatively high-intensity program. In FY2011 on average, Regular UB, UBMS, and VUB projects expended $4,697, $4,836, and $2,280 per participant, respectively.[8] The Regular UB and UBMS per-participant spending is, on average, at least 10 times more than TS and EOC projects, which may also serve secondary school students.

The HEA requires each grantee to provide the following seven services:

- instruction in mathematics through precalculus, laboratory science, foreign language, composition, and literature, as part of the core curriculum in the third and succeeding years;[9]
- academic tutoring to enable students to complete secondary or postsecondary courses;
- secondary and postsecondary course selection advice and assistance;
- assistance in preparing for college entrance examinations and assistance in completing college admission applications;

---

[5] The HEOA amendments clarified that community based organizations were eligible to receive grants.

[6] Prior to the HEOA, secondary schools were eligible in *exceptional circumstances*.

[7] Prior to the HEOA, the remaining one-third of participants were either low-income or first-generation college.

[8] FY2013 President's Budget Request.

[9] Although some grantees such as high schools may already offer these instructional services to UB participants and other students, other grantees must include these instructional services as part of the core curriculum.

- information on student financial aid opportunities and assistance in completing financial aid applications;
- guidance on and assistance in methods for achieving a secondary school diploma or an equivalent or postsecondary education; and
- education or counseling services designed to improve financial and economic literacy.

Per regulations, Regular UB and UBMS grantees must provide a summer instructional component. Regulations also require UBMS grantees to provide participants with opportunities to learn from mathematicians and scientists who are engaged in research and teaching and opportunities with graduate and undergraduate science and mathematics majors.

Program statute lists permissible activities such as exposure to cultural events, academic programs not usually available to disadvantaged students and mentoring programs, and programs and activities designed specifically for special populations.[10] Program regulations allow UB grantees, under certain conditions, to pay tuition for courses that will allow participants to complete a rigorous secondary school program of study and room and board for a residential summer instructional component.

Regular UB and UBMS grantees may also provide such services as cultural or academic field trips, mentoring, work-study, or stipends. The Regular UB and UBMS stipends may not exceed $40 per month for the academic year component and may not exceed $60 per month for the three-month summer recess, except that youth participating in work-study may be paid $300 per month during the summer recess. Regular UB and UBMS stipends are for full-time, *satisfactory* participants only.[11]

VUB grantees may provide such services as short-term remedial or refresher courses, stipends, and assistance accessing veteran support services. The VUB stipend may not exceed $40 per month and is for full-time, satisfactory participants only.

Outcome Criteria

All UB projects must annually report the extent to which they meet or exceed the goals approved in their application for the following outcome criteria:

- the number of participants served;
- participant school performance, as measured by the percentage of participants with a specified cumulative grade point average (inapplicable to VUB grantees);
- participant academic performance, as measured by the percentage of participants scoring at or above the proficient level on state standardized tests in

---

[10] Special populations include students who are limited English proficient, students from groups that are traditionally underrepresented in postsecondary education, students with disabilities, students who are homeless children and youths students who are in foster care or are aging out of the foster care system, and other disconnected students.

[11] Satisfactory participation is defined in regulations as having regular program attendance and performing in accordance with standards established by the grantee and described in the application.

reading/language arts and math, or, in the case of VUB, receiving a better score on a standardized test after completing the program;

- secondary school retention and graduation of participants, as measured by the percentage of participants re-enrolling at the next grade level or graduating with a regular high school diploma or, in the case of VUB, program retention or completion;

- completion of a rigorous secondary school curriculum (see box below), as measured by the percentage of current and prior participants expected to graduate who actually graduate with a regular high school diploma and complete a rigorous secondary school curriculum (inapplicable to VUB grantees);

- postsecondary enrollment of participants, as measured by the percentage of current and prior participants expected to graduate or, in the case of VUB, who have completed the VUB program and enrolled in an IHE within a specified timeframe; and

- completion of a postsecondary degree, as measured by the percentage of prior participants enrolled in an IHE within a specified timeframe who graduate with a degree within a specified period or, in the case of VUB, completion of postsecondary education.

Rigorous Secondary School Program of Study

A rigorous secondary school program of study is defined in regulations as a program of study that is

- recognized as such for the no-longer-funded Academic Competitiveness Grant (ACG) Program (HEA section 401A);

- an advanced or honors program established by the state;

- any program in which a student successfully completes at least four years of English; three years of mathematics, including algebra I and a higher-level class; three years of science, including one year each of at least two of the following courses: biology, chemistry, and physics; three years of social studies; and one year of a language other than English;

- a program identified by a state-level partnership that is recognized by the no-longer-funded State Scholars Initiative;

- any program for a student who completes at least two courses from an International Baccalaureate (IB) Diploma Program and receives a score of a "4" or higher on the examinations for at least two of those courses; or

- any program for a student who completes at least two Advanced Placement (AP) courses and receives a score of "3" or higher on the AP exams for at least two of those courses.

TRIO Talent Search (TS) Program[12]

The TS program also has the aim of high school completion and postsecondary enrollment. It encourages students to complete high school and enroll in postsecondary education; helps students apply for student financial assistance; and encourages older individuals who have not completed secondary or postsecondary education to enter, or re-enter, and complete such programs.

---

[12] HEA section 402B; 20 U.S.C. §1070a-12; 34 C.F.R. 643.

Eligible Recipients

Grants or contracts are available to institutions of higher education (IHEs); public and private agencies and organizations, including community-based organizations (CBOs) with experience in serving disadvantaged youth;[13] secondary schools;[14] and combinations of such institutions, agencies, and organizations.

Program Participants

All participants must have completed five years of elementary education or be at least 11 years of age but not more than 27 years of age, unless the age and grade limitation defeats the purpose of the program. Individuals over 27 may participate if they cannot be served by an area Educational Opportunity Centers (EOC) grantee. At least two-thirds of the program participants must be low-income, first-generation college students. For each new grant competition after 2010, the secretary identifies the minimum number of participants and the minimum and maximum grant award amounts in the *Federal Register* notice inviting applications.[15]

Program Intensity and Activities

Grantees must provide course selection advice and assistance, assistance in preparing for college entrance examinations, assistance in completing college admission applications, information on student financial aid opportunities, assistance in completing financial aid applications, and guidance on and assistance in methods for achieving a secondary school diploma or an equivalent or postsecondary education. Because TS is a less intensive program than UB, grantees need only provide connections to tutoring and connections to services designed to improve financial and economic literacy. The list of required services, as amended by the HEOA, requires TS grantees to provide a fuller range of services and more intensive services than prior to the HEOA. The average cost per TS participant increased from about $393 in FY2008–FY2010 to $434 in FY2011, the first year of a new grant cycle under the HEOA.

Examples of permissible activities are exposure to cultural events, academic programs not usually available to disadvantaged students, mentoring programs, tutoring, counseling, exposure to careers or higher education, and related programs and activities designed specifically for special populations.[16] Program regulations permit grantees to pay for tuition, transportation, meals, and, if necessary, lodging, for participants and staff in limited situations because TS is designed as a low cost per participant program. Under limited circumstances, program regulations allow the TS grantees to pay participant educational costs, such as transportation, meals, high school equivalency programs, college applications, and college entrance examinations but not third-party college entrance exam preparation.

---

[13] The HEOA amendments clarified that community based organizations were eligible to receive grants.

[14] Prior to the HEOA, secondary schools were eligible in *exceptional circumstances*.

[15] Prior to the HEOA by regulation, grantees had to serve a minimum of 600 participants in each budget period.

[16] Special populations include students who are limited English proficient, students from groups that are traditionally underrepresented in postsecondary education, students with disabilities, students who are homeless children and youths students who are in foster care or are aging out of the foster care system, and other disconnected students.

Outcome Criteria

All TS projects must annually report the extent to which they meet or exceed the goals approved in their application for the following statutory outcome criteria:

- the number of participants served;
- the secondary school retention of participants;
- the graduation of participants with a regular secondary school diploma in the standard number of years;
- the graduation of participants having completed a rigorous secondary school curriculum;
- the postsecondary enrollment of participants; and
- the postsecondary education completion of participants.

TRIO Educational Opportunity Centers (EOC) Program[17]

Like Upward Bound (UB) and Talent Search (TS), the EOC program also supports high school completion and postsecondary enrollment. EOC provides information on financial and academic assistance available to individuals who want to pursue postsecondary education; provides assistance in applying for admission to postsecondary education and assistance in completing financial aid applications; and improves the financial and economic literacy of students.

Eligible Recipients

Grants or contracts are available to IHEs; public and private agencies and organizations, including CBOs with experience in serving disadvantaged youth;[18] secondary schools;[19] and combinations of such institutions, agencies, and organizations.

Program Participants

All participants must be at least 19 years of age, unless the age limitation defeats the purpose of the program. One prominent distinction between the TS and EOC programs is that EOC grantees generally serve an adult population; however, TS may serve adults and EOC may serve secondary-age students if the individuals cannot be appropriately served by the other program and if the individual's participation does not dilute the project's services. In addition, at least two-thirds of the program participants must be low-income, first-generation college students.

Program Intensity and Activities

EOC projects provide the least intensive services as measured by the $248 cost per participant in FY2011.[20] Unlike the other student-serving TRIO programs, EOC statutory provisions do not

---

[17] HEA section 402F; 20 U.S.C. §1070a-16; 34 C.F.R. 644.

[18] The HEOA amendments clarified that community based organizations were eligible to receive grants.

[19] Prior to the HEOA, secondary schools were eligible in *exceptional circumstances*.

establish activities required of all grantees. Grantees may provide such services as academic advice and assistance in course selection, tutoring, public information campaigns regarding postsecondary education opportunities, and counseling and guidance. The EOC projects may also provide programs and activities designed specifically for special populations.[21] Program regulations allow spending on transportation, meals, and, with specific prior approval of the secretary, lodging under limited circumstances because the EOC program is intended to have a low cost per participant. Program regulations also allow grantees to pay for college applications, college entrance examinations, and examination fees for alternative education programs.

Outcome Criteria

All EOC projects must annually report the extent to which they meet or exceed the goals approved in their application for the following statutory outcome criteria:

- The total number of program participants;
- The completion of a secondary school diploma or its recognized equivalent by participants that did not have a secondary school diploma or its recognized equivalent;
- The enrollment of secondary school graduates who were served by the program in programs of postsecondary education;
- The number of participants completing financial aid applications; and
- The number of participants applying for college admission.

Prior to the HEOA, the secretary awarded PE points per regulations based on the number of participants; participant demographics; the provision of assistance in applying for admission to, or financial aid for, programs of postsecondary education; and the admission or reentry of participants to postsecondary education.

TRIO Student Support Services (SSS) Program[22]

The SSS program provides support services to college students with the aim of improving their retention, graduation rates, financial and economic literacy, and transfers from two-year to four-year schools. SSS programs are also intended to foster an institutional climate supportive of potentially disconnected students.[23]

(...continued)

[20] FY2013 President's Budget Request.

[21] Special populations include students who are limited English proficient, students from groups that are traditionally underrepresented in postsecondary education, students with disabilities, students who are homeless children and youths students who are in foster care or are aging out of the foster care system, and other disconnected students.

[22] HEA section 402D; 20 U.S.C. §1070a-14; 34 C.F.R. 646.

[23] Disconnected students include students who are limited English proficient, students from groups that are traditionally underrepresented in postsecondary education, students with disabilities, students who are homeless children and youths, and students who are in foster care or are aging out of the foster care system.

Eligible Recipients

Grants or contracts are available to IHEs and combinations of IHEs.

Program Participants

All SSS participants must be enrolled, or accepted for enrollment, at the grantee and be in need of academic support to pursue education successfully beyond secondary school. At least two-thirds of participants must be either students with disabilities[24] or low-income, first-generation college students. The remaining one-third of participants must be low-income, first-generation college, or students with disabilities. Also, at least one-third of the participating students with disabilities must be low-income.

Program Intensity and Activities

In FY2006, SSS projects expended $1,347 per participant, on average.[25] All TRIO SSS programs must offer

- academic tutoring, directly or through other institutional services;
- course selection advice and assistance;
- assistance in preparing for college entrance examinations;
- assistance in completing college admission applications;
- education or counseling services designed to improve financial and economic literacy;
- information on student financial aid opportunities and assistance in completing financial aid applications; and
- assistance in applying for admission to, and obtaining financial assistance for enrollment in, either graduate and professional programs to students enrolled in four-year IHEs or four-year programs of postsecondary education to students enrolled in two-year IHEs.

In addition to the required services, grantees may also provide services such as academic or career counseling, exposure to cultural events, academic programs not usually available to disadvantaged students, mentoring programs, temporary housing for homeless and foster care youth, related programs and activities designed specifically for special populations,[26] and student aid stipends. Program regulations allow grantees to provide transportation and, with prior

---

[24] For the purpose of all the TRIO programs and since October 2010, an individual with a disability is a person with a disability, as that term is defined in section 12102 of the Americans with Disabilities Act (ADA; 42 U.S.C. 12101 et seq.). Prior to October 2010, program regulations defined "individual with disabilities [as] a person who has a diagnosed physical or mental impairment that substantially limits that person's ability to participate in the educational experiences and opportunities offered by the grantee institution."

[25] FY2008 President's Budget Request.

[26] Special populations include students who are limited English proficient, students from groups that are traditionally underrepresented in postsecondary education, students with disabilities, students who are homeless children and youths students who are in foster care or are aging out of the foster care system, and other disconnected students.

approval of the secretary, meals and lodging for participants and staff during approved educational and cultural activities sponsored by the project. Program regulations limit expenditures on professional development travel to no more than 4% of staff salaries.

Projects may provide student aid stipends to program participants who are in the first two years of postsecondary education and who are receiving Pell Grants.[27] If the needs of Pell-recipient SSS program participants in the first two years of postsecondary education are fulfilled, projects may also provide student aid stipends to Pell-recipient SSS program participants who have completed the first two years of postsecondary education and who are at high risk of dropping out. Student aid stipends must be greater than 10% of the total maximum Pell Grant award amount but no more than the sum of the discretionary base maximum Pell award and add-on Pell award as determined for each student.[28] Grantees may not use more than 20% of their SSS award for student aid stipends and must match at least one-half of the federal funds used for SSS student aid stipends, in cash, from non-federal sources unless the IHE is eligible for Title III-A, Title III-B, or Title V of the HEA. Title III-A, Title III-B, and Title V of the HEA provide institutional aid to IHEs with lower than average educational and general expenditures and high enrollments of needy students and to historically Black colleges and universities (HBCUs).

Outcome Criteria

All SSS projects must annually report the extent to which they meet or exceed the goals approved in their application for the following statutory outcome criteria:

- The number of participants;
- Participant postsecondary retention, completion, or transfer from a two-year to four-year IHE;
- The participants who remain in good academic standing;
- For two-year IHEs, the completion of a degree or certificate and the transfer to baccalaureate degree-granting IHEs; and
- For baccalaureate degree-granting IHEs, the percentage of students completing the degree programs in which enrolled.

Prior to the HEOA, the secretary awarded prior experience points per regulations based on participant postsecondary persistence, participants being in good academic standing, participant graduation from four-year IHEs or graduation from two-year IHEs and transfer from two-year to four-year IHEs, and projects meeting the program administrative requirements.

---

[27] For more information on Pell Grants, see CRS Report R42446, *Federal Pell Grant Program of the Higher Education Act: How the Program Works, Recent Legislative Changes, and Current Issues*, by Shannon M. Mahan, pp. 4-12.

[28] An SSS student aid stipend shall not be considered in determining that student's need for grant or work assistance under Title IV of the HEA, but the total amount of student financial assistance awarded to a student under Title IV of the HEA cannot exceed that student's cost of attendance.

Ronald E. McNair Postbaccalaureate Achievement (McNair) Program[29]

The TRIO McNair program helps prepare disadvantaged college students for subsequent doctoral study by providing research opportunities, internships, counseling, tutoring, and other preparatory activities.

Eligible Recipients

Grants or contracts are available to IHEs and combinations of IHEs.

Program Participants

All participants must be enrolled in a degree program at the grantee. At least two-thirds of students served must be low-income, first-generation college students. The remaining one-third of participants must be from a group that is underrepresented in graduate education, including Alaska Natives, Native Hawaiians, and Native American Pacific Islanders.

Program Intensity and Activities

In FY2011, on average, McNair projects expended $8,511 per participant.[30] All projects must provide academic tutoring, academic counseling, summer internships that prepare participants for doctoral study, opportunities for research or other scholarly activities, seminars and other educational activities designed to prepare students for doctoral study, and assistance in securing graduate program admissions and financial assistance. Projects may provide stipends of no more than $2,800 annually and the costs of summer tuition, summer room and board, and transportation to students engaged in summer research internships, provided that the student has completed the sophomore year before the internship begins. Projects may also provide services such as mentoring programs, exposure to cultural events and academic programs, and services designed to improve financial and economic literacy.

Outcome Criteria

All McNair projects must annually report the extent to which they meet or exceed the goals approved in their application for the following statutory outcome criteria:

- The total number of program participants;
- The provision of appropriate scholarly or research activities for participants;
- The acceptance and enrollment of participants in graduate programs;
- The retention of prior participants in graduate study, and
- The attainment of doctoral degrees by prior participants.

---

[29] HEA section 402E; 20 U.S.C. §1070a-15; 34 C.F.R. 647.
[30] FY2013 President's Budget Request.

TRIO Staff Development (Training) Program[31]

The TRIO Training program provides training to existing and potential TRIO program staff to improve project administration, operation, outcomes, and outreach.

Eligible Recipients

Two-year grants or contracts are available to IHEs and public and private nonprofit institutions and organizations. Grantees may receive more than one award if the additional awards are intended to meet different absolute priorities established for the competition. ED includes an absolute priority in a grant competition to focus the competition on specific objectives or activities, and each applicant must address the absolute priority to be eligible for funding.

Program Participants

Program participants are staff and leadership personnel employed in, participating in, or preparing for employment in, TRIO programs and projects.

Program Intensity and Activities

Grantees provide annual training through conferences, internships, seminars, workshops, and manuals designed to improve TRIO programs. Allowable costs include transportation and lodging of participants, staff, and consultants and honorariums for speakers. Training is designed specifically for new TRIO project directors and designed to cover specific topics such as legislative and regulatory requirements, the use of educational technology, or strategies for recruiting disconnected students. ED establishes absolute priorities to ensure the desired populations and specific topics are covered in each grant competition. At least one grantee will train new TRIO project directors. At least one grantee will cover the specific topics listed in the application notice. ED also ensures that training is offered in every geographic region and customized to local needs.

Outcome Criteria

Unlike the student-serving TRIO programs, there are no statutorily defined outcome criteria for the Training program. Program regulations require all Training projects to annually report the extent to which they meet or exceed the goals approved in their application for the following outcome criteria:

- The number of participants served;
- Assisting participants in developing increased qualifications and skills to meet the needs of disadvantaged students;
- Providing the participants with an increased knowledge and understanding of the TRIO programs; and
- The applicant meeting all administrative requirements.

---

[31] HEA section 402G; 20 U.S.C. §1070a-17; 34 C.F.R. 642.

Comparison of Key Features of the TRIO Programs

A comparison of program features and eligible participants across the TRIO programs follows.

Table 1. TRIO Program Eligible Grant Recipients

Eligible Grant Recipients	Upward Bound	Talent Search	Educational Opportunity Centers	Student Support Services	Ronald E. McNair Postbaccalaureate Achievement	Staff Development
Institutions of higher education (IHEs)	X	X	X	X	X	X
Public and private agencies and organizations	X	X	X			X
Secondary schools	X	X	X			
Combinations of the above institutions, agencies, and organizations	X	X	X	X	X	

Source: Table prepared by CRS based on statutory and regulatory provisions.

Table 2. Comparison of the Required Program Participant Demographics across the TRIO Programs

Program	Age/Grade Range	Additional	>= 2/3rd of Participants	Remaining 1/3rd of Participants
Upward Bound	After eight years of elementary education or 13-19 years of age[a]	In need of academic support to pursue education beyond secondary school successfully	Low-income, first-generation college students	Low-income, first-generation college, or at-risk of academic failure[b] for Regular Upward Bound and Veterans Upward Bound or low-income or first-generation college for Upward Bound Math-Science
Talent Search	After five years of elementary education or 11-27 years of age[a]	Over 27 years of age if Educational Opportunity Centers not accessible	Low-income, first-generation college students	NA
Educational Opportunity Centers	>= 19 years of age[a]	Under 19 years of age if Talent Search not accessible	Low-income, first-generation college students	NA
Student Support Services	Enrolled or accepted for enrollment at grantee institution	In need of academic support to pursue education beyond secondary school successfully	Low-income, first-generation college students or students with disabilities	Low-income, first-generation college, or students with disabilities

Program	Age/Grade Range	Additional	>= 2/3rd of Participants	Remaining 1/3rd of Participants
Ronald E. McNair Postbaccalaureate Achievement	Enrolled in a degree program at grantee institution	NA	Low-income, first-generation college students	Underrepresented in graduate education
Staff Development	NA	Potential and current TRIO staff and leadership personnel	NA	NA

Source: Table prepared by CRS based on statutory provisions.

Notes: NA means not applicable.

a. The age and grade range requirements are applicable unless the age and grade limitation defeats the purpose of the program.

b. A Regular UB individual who has a high risk for academic failure is not at the proficient level on state assessments in reading or language arts; is not at the proficient level on state assessments in math; has not successfully completed pre-algebra or algebra by the beginning of the 10th grade; or has a grade point average of 2.5 or less (on a 4.0 scale) for the most recent school year. A veteran who has a high risk for academic failure has been out of high school or dropped out of a program of postsecondary education for five or more years; has scored on standardized tests below the level that demonstrates a likelihood of success in a program of postsecondary education; or meets the definition of an individual with a disability.

Table 3. Comparison of the Required Program Activities for the Student Serving TRIO Programs

Required Activity	Upward Bound	Talent Search	Educational Opportunity Centers[a]	Student Support Services	Ronald E. McNair Postbaccalaureate Achievement
Assistance with college entrance examinations and admission applications	X	X		X	X
Information on financial aid opportunities and assistance in completing financial aid applications	X	X		X[b]	X
Academic tutoring	X	X[c]		X	X
Course selection advice and assistance	X	X		X	
Services to improve financial and economic literacy	X	X[c]		X	
Guidance on and assistance in methods for achieving a secondary school diploma or an equivalent or postsecondary education	X	X			
Academic instruction	X				
Summer component	X[d]				X[e]
Research and teaching and opportunities	X[f]				X[g]
Seminars and activities designed to prepare students for doctoral study					X
Academic counseling					X

Source: Table prepared by CRS based on statutory and regulatory provisions.

The TRIO Programs

a. Educational Opportunity Centers' statutory provisions do not establish activities required of all grantees.
b. Student Support Services' grantees must provide assistance in applying for admission to, and obtaining financial assistance for enrollment in, either graduate and professional programs to students enrolled in four-year institutions of higher education (IHEs) or four-year programs of postsecondary education to students enrolled in two-year IHEs.
c. Talent Search grantees need only provide connections to tutoring and connections to services designed to improve financial and economic literacy.
d. Upward Bound and Upward Bound Math-Science regulations require that grantees provide a summer instructional component.
e. The Ronald E. McNair Postbaccalaureate Achievement summer component is internships that prepare participants for doctoral study.
f. Regulations require Upward Bound Math-Science grantees to provide participants with opportunities to learn from mathematicians and scientists who are engaged in research and teaching and opportunities with graduate and undergraduate science and mathematics majors.
g. Ronald E. McNair Postbaccalaureate Achievement projects must provide opportunities for research or other scholarly activities.

Program Appropriations and Project Participants

The Higher Education Act (HEA), as amended, authorized a total of $700 million for the TRIO programs for FY1999 and such sums as necessary for each of FY2000-FY2003.[32] The authorization of appropriations is intended to provide guidance regarding the appropriate amount of funds to carry out the authorized activities of a program. The Higher Education Opportunity Act (HEOA; P.L. 110-315) of 2008 raised the authorization level to a total of $900 million for FY2009 and such sums as necessary for each of FY2010-FY2014. Of the TRIO authorization, McNair is authorized at least $11 million for each of FY2009-FY2014.

The annual *discretionary* appropriation is a single amount for all of the TRIO programs. The appropriation provides budget authority to the U.S. Department of Education to incur obligations and authorize payments for the specified programs. The annual appropriation increased from $828 million in FY2006 to $853 million in FY2010 before declining to $827 million in FY2011 and $840 million in FY2012. The secretary allocates the discretionary appropriation to the various TRIO programs. **Table 4** displays appropriations and allocations over the latest 10 year period.

Through the College Cost Reduction and Access Act (CCRAA; P.L. 110-84), ED received a *mandatory* appropriation of $57 million for each of FY2008-FY2011 to make four-year awards to 186 unsuccessful UB applicants from the FY2007 competition that scored above 70.[33] The mandatory funding was appropriated, in part, to fund several historically Black colleges and universities that lost their awards in the FY2007 competition.[34]

---

[32] The program was not authorized from FY2003 to FY2008, but Congress continued to appropriate funds.

[33] Funds in excess of those needed to fund UB awards were permitted to be expended on UB program administration and technical assistance.

[34] Kelly Field, "Changes Debated for Upward Bound," *The Chronicle of Higher Education*, July 6, 2007.

Table 4. TRIO Appropriations and Program Allocations: FY2006-FY2012

($ in millions)

TRIO Programs and Spending	FY2003	FY2004	FY2005	FY2006	FY2007	FY2008	FY2009	FY2010	FY2011	FY2012
Discretionary Appropriations										
Talent Search	145	144	145	150	143	143	142	142	139	136
Upward Bound	279	287	277	267	267	259	257	257	249	266
Veterans Upward Bound	NR[a]	NR[a]	NR[a]	12	13	12	14	14	13	13
Upward Bound Math-Science	34	33	33	32	34	31	35	35	34	44
Educational Opportunity Centers	48	49	49	48	47	47	47	47	48	47
Student Support Services	264	263	278	271	272	284	302	302	291	291
Ronald E. McNair Postbaccalaureate Achievement	42	42	42	42	45	45	47	48	46	36
Staff Development	8	5	5	3	3	3	3	4	4	1
Evaluation	2	1	1	1	2	0	—	1	0	2
Administrative expenses	3	3	3	3	2	3	1	4	4	3
Subtotal	827	833	837	828	828	828	848	853	827	840
Upward Bound (Mandatory)[b]	-	-	-	-	-	57	57	57	57	—
Total TRIO	827	833	837	828	828	885	905	910	884	840

Source: U.S. Department of Education Budget Requests, FY2005-FY2013.

Notes: Totals may not add due to rounding, and table excludes funds allocated to Dissemination Partnership Grants. Dissemination Partnership Grants supported partnerships between TRIO grantees and institutions of higher education and community-based organizations that did not receive TRIO grant funds but served low-income, first-generation students. Continuation grants were made under the Dissemination Partnership Grants program from FY2003 to FY2005 in the amount of approximately $4 million annually.

a. NR means not reported separately. Funding for Veterans Upward Bound projects is included in Upward Bound and Upward Bound Math-Science totals.

b. The authorization for mandatory funding of $57 million for each of fiscal years 2008 to 2011 were made available by the College Cost Reduction and Access Act (CCRAA; P.L. 110-84) to make four-year awards to 186 unsuccessful Upward Bound applicants for the FY2007 competition who scored above an average peer review score of 70 out of 115 points. Any funds not needed for grants may be used for technical assistance and administration costs for the Upward Bound program.

The TRIO programs served over 820,000 participants in each of FY2008-FY2010 (**Table 5**). In FY2011, the TRIO programs served fewer than 790,000 participants as a result of a reduction in the number of TS participants. The number of TS participants declined, in part, as a result of ED reducing the TS allocation from $142 million in FY2010 to $139 million in FY2011 and establishing $460 as the maximum cost per participant in the FY2011 competition in response to the HEOA amendments, which increased the intensity of TS services. TRIO participation data reflects the number of participants served by each program. The intensity of services received and the duration of participation differs for each program and among individuals in the same program.

Table 5. Number of TRIO Participants: FY2008-FY2011

TRIO Programs	FY2008	FY2009	FY2010	FY2011
Talent Search (TS)	363,300	361,179	359,740	319,678
Upward Bound (UB)	53,690	53,531	53,333	53,184
Veterans Upward Bound (VUB)	5,060	5,900	5,780	5,780
Upward Bound Math-Science (UBMS)	6,250	7,057	7,007	6,992
Educational Opportunity Centers (EOC)	195,795	194,795	194,445	192,196
Student Support Services (SSS)	198,940	197,439	204,181	202,921
McNair Post Baccalaureate (McNair)	5,067	5,439	5,430	5,419
UB Mandatory funding	11,489	11,598	11,192	11,078
Total	**828,102**	**825,340**	**829,916**	**786,170**

Source: President's Budget Request, FY2010-FY2013.

Major HEOA Amendments to Common TRIO Provisions

Several statutory provisions common to most of the TRIO programs were amended or added by the Higher Education Opportunity Act (HEOA; P.L. 110-315) of 2008. The HEOA made several important changes to the grant making process, which impact the way the Department of Education (ED) administers the programs and the way grantees implement their funds. Through the HEOA, Congress also attempted to standardize the grant cycle and maximize the numbers of disadvantaged students participating.

Required Program Activities

TRIO services support the goals of secondary school completion, college preparation, college enrollment, undergraduate completion, and graduate school preparation. Prior to the HEOA, statutory provisions identified only a list of permissible services for each of the programs. With the exception of EOC, the HEOA defined a list of required services and a list of permissible services for each program. The required services are expected to increase consistency across grantees, and it is hoped that this will increase program effectiveness. All of the required services must be made available to all program participants; however, not all participants may need nor choose to avail themselves of the required services. In other words, the required services must be offered by the program, but participants have the ability to choose which services they receive.

Grantees may offer services that are not listed explicitly as required or permissible as long as the services further the purpose of the program. The required activities are described in the relevant program sections above and presented for the student-serving programs in **Table 3**.

Prior Experience Points

The TRIO programs have always been designed to reward successful grantees with new grants. In making new discretionary grants, ED employs peer reviewers who have relevant background and expertise to read and evaluate grant applications. The peer reviewers score each application up to 100 points based on a set of selection criteria. For the student-serving TRIO programs, statutory provisions have also required ED to consider each applicant's *prior experience* of service delivery by allowing prior grantees to earn additional prior experience (PE) points. Grants are then awarded in rank order on the basis of the applications' total score—peer review score plus PE points.

PE points have been awarded according to the extent to which a student-serving TRIO program grantee meets or exceeds the objectives in its prior application. Program regulations prior to passage of the HEOA required that grantees propose *ambitious but attainable* objectives for the outcome criteria that were defined in regulations. The outcome criteria were primarily based on measures related to the number of participants served and their academic achievements or the services of which they took advantage. The extent to which the grantee met or exceeded its prior grant objectives determined how many of the 15 possible PE points applicants received in the competition.

Prior to the HEOA during the FY2006 TS and EOC competitions, several applicants charged that they were denied funding because ED did not apply PE points uniformly and according to its regulations. ED's Office of Inspector General (OIG) found that ED had improperly awarded PE points by not complying with its regulations, awarding PE points to applicants that did not meet minimum requirements, making execution errors, and changing the process.[35] The OIG also found that ED did not have a well-defined, transparent process for reviewing grantee performance and did not hold grantees responsible for serving fewer participants than funded to serve.[36]

Congress through the HEOA desired to increase the rigor, quality, effectiveness, and accountability of the TRIO student-serving programs by establishing outcome criteria on which to base PE points for each of the student-serving programs (see **Table 6**).[37] The Secretary and applicant agree upon targets/objectives for each of the outcome criteria, as defined by statute and refined in regulations and Federal Register notices. Statutory provisions also require that the outcome criteria measure the quality and effectiveness of projects annually and over multiple

---

[35] U.S. Department of Education, Office of Inspector General, *Review of the Office of Postsecondary Education's Awarding of Prior Experience Points in the 2006 Educational Opportunity Centers and Talent Search Grant Competitions: Final Inspection Report*, ED-OIG/I13I0001, Washington, DC, September 8, 2008.

[36] U.S. Department of Education, Office of Inspector General, *Review of the Office of Postsecondary Education's Actions to Address Talent Search and Educational Opportunity Centers Grantees That Did Not Serve the Number of Participants They Were Funded to Serve in Fiscal Years 2003-07*, ED-OIG/I13I0007, Washington, DC, September 30, 2009.

[37] U.S. Congress, House Committee on Education and Labor, *College Opportunity and Affordability Act of 2007*, 110th Cong., 1st sess., December 19, 2007, H.Rept. 110-500.

years. By regulation, prior grantees that failed to serve at least 90% of the approved number of participants do not receive any PE points.

Table 6. Statutory Outcome Criteria for the Student-Serving TRIO Programs

Outcome Criteria[a]	Upward Bound	Talent Search	Educational Opportunity Centers	Student Support Services	Ronald E. McNair Postbaccalaureate Achievement
Number of participants served	X	X	X	X	X
Secondary school education					
Secondary education enrollment			X		
Secondary school retention		X			
School performance, as measured by grade point average or the equivalent	X				
Academic performance, as measured by standardized tests	X				
Secondary school retention and graduation	X				
Secondary school graduation with a regular diploma in the standard number of years		X			
Completion of a rigorous secondary school program of study	X	X			
Undergraduate postsecondary education					
Assistance completing financial aid applications and college admission applications			X		
Postsecondary enrollment		X	X		
Postsecondary enrollment in an institution of higher education	X				
Good academic standing				X	
Postsecondary retention				X	
Postsecondary completion	X	X			
Degree/certificate completion at two-year IHE and transfer to four-year IHE				X	
Degree completion at four-year IHE				X	
Provision of appropriate scholarly and research activities					X
Graduate postsecondary education					
Graduate school acceptance and enrollment					X
Graduate school retention and doctoral degree attainment					X

Source: Table prepared by CRS based on Title IV-A-2-1 of the Higher Education Act, as amended, and 34 C.F.R. 642-647.

a. The Secretary further refines the outcome criteria through regulations and through *Federal Register* notices for each grant competition.

Some of the outcome criteria raised program expectations above those established in regulations prior to the HEOA. For instance prior to the HEOA, TS outcome criteria focused on participant numbers, participant demographics, high school retention and completion, and postsecondary enrollment. The HEOA added criteria for the completion of a rigorous secondary school program of education and postsecondary completion. Also prior to the HEOA, the Secretary awarded PE points for UB based on the number of participants served; participants' improvement on standardized achievement tests and grade point averages (GPAs); UB program retention; postsecondary enrollment; and postsecondary education success. The HEOA and regulations revised the criterion of improvement on standardized tests to achievement on standardized tests, revised the criterion of postsecondary success to postsecondary completion, and added a criterion for participants' completing a rigorous secondary program of education. Grant competitions for FY2011 and beyond, following passage of the HEOA and final regulations, use the outcome criteria established by the HEOA.

TRIO Training uses a different process for PE points, and it was not amended by the HEOA. ED awards Training applicants based on the peer review score ranking compared to other applicants that address the same absolute priority (see the section on Required Program Activities). ED uses PE points in case of a tie in the peer review scores. PE points are awarded per regulations to prior grantees on the basis of their established objectives on

- The number of participants served;
- Assisting participants in developing increased qualifications and skills to meet the needs of disadvantaged students;
- Providing the participants with an increased knowledge and understanding of the TRIO programs; and
- The applicant meeting all administrative requirements.

Application Review Process (Appeal)

Also in response to the OIG report finding that ED improperly awarded PE points and evidence of other errors by ED in processing applications,[38] the HEOA added provisions allowing certain unsuccessful applicants to request a second review of their application, sometimes referred to as an appeal. To be eligible for a second review, the applicant must have evidence of a specific technical, administrative, or scoring error made by ED or a peer reviewer with respect to the scoring or processing of a submitted application, and the applicant must have otherwise met all of the application submission requirements. According to statute to the extent feasible based on the availability of appropriations, the secretary will fund applications with scores adjusted as a result of a second review if the scores are equal to or exceed the minimum cut score for the competition.

Per regulations, the secretary reserves a portion of the appropriation to award grants under the second review. Under ED regulations, the only applicants eligible for a second review are those that were not funded under the first review but that had an application score that could be funded

---

[38] U.S. Congress, House of Representatives, *Higher Education Opportunity Act*, Conference Report to accompany H.R. 4137, 110th Cong., 2nd sess., July 30, 2008, H.Rept. 110-803 (Washington: GPO, 2008), p. 505.

if the secretary had reserved 150% of the appropriation actually reserved to fund under the second review. During the FY2012 Regular UB competition, the secretary reserved almost $9 million (3.5%) of the over $260 million allocation for the second review.

Award Amounts and Numbers of Program Participants

Statutory provisions establish a minimum grant award of $200,000 for the student-serving TRIO programs, unless the applicant requests a smaller amount, and $170,000 for the Training program.[39] Per regulations for each new grant competition after 2010, the secretary identifies the minimum number of participants and the minimum and maximum grant award amounts in the Federal Register notice inviting applications.[40]

For example for the FY2011 TS grant competition, the secretary required all applicants to propose serving at least 500 participants for no more than $460 per participant. *New grantees* were eligible to receive an award of up to $230,000. *Prior grantees* were allowed a maximum award of the greater of $230,000 or 103% of their prior award amount.

Prior to the HEOA, the statutory minimum award for UB was $190,000. The secretary regulated the number of participants each project had to serve, unless the applicant demonstrated that the project would be more cost effective and consistent with the objectives of the program. Regular UB projects were expected to serve 50-150 participants; UBMS projects were expected to serve 50-75 participants; and VUB projects were expected to serve at least 120 participants. Thus, the secretary essentially established a base cost per participant of $1,267-$3,800 for Regular UB, $2,533-$3,800 for UBMS, and $1,583 for VUB.

Length of Grant Award

The student-serving TRIO program grants are awarded for a period of five years. Training grants are awarded for a period of two years. Prior to the HEOA, student-serving TRIO program grants were awarded for a period of five years to applicants scoring in the highest 10% and for a period of four years for all other applicants. The HEOA allowed the secretary a one-time, limited extension of grants to synchronize all of the grants on the same schedule. The secretary extended the SSS projects scheduled to end in 2009 until 2010; the TS and EOC projects scheduled to end in 2010 until 2011; and the UB and McNair projects scheduled to end in 2011 until 2012. These extensions, however, did not synchronize the grant periods.

Multiple Grants for Different Populations

Some Members of Congress were concerned that ED regulations prevented the TRIO programs from serving the maximum number of disadvantaged students.[41] The HEOA added a provision

---

[39] Prior to the HEOA, the statutory minimum award was $170,000 for SSS and Training; $180,000 for TS and EOC, and $190,000 for UB and McNair.

[40] Prior to the HEOA, regulations established a minimum of number of participants in each budget period for UB, TS, and EOC.

[41] U.S. Congress, House Committee on Education and Labor, *College Opportunity and Affordability Act of 2007*, 110th Cong., 1st sess., December 19, 2007, H.Rept. 110-500.

clarifying that grantees may receive more than one award if the additional awards serve different populations, target areas, target schools, or different campuses. The secretary publishes the *different populations* for which an eligible entity may submit a separate application for each grant competition. Applicants that propose serving a different population from the prior grant do not receive PE points for the application serving a new population. Prior to the HEOA, this had been allowed to varying degrees by program regulations.

In the FY2010 SSS grant competition, the secretary defined six different populations: (1) participants who meet the minimum SSS requirements; (2) participants with disabilities exclusively; (3) English as a second language (ESL) participants exclusively; (4) participants receiving services in the science, technology, engineering, and mathematics (STEM) fields; (5) participants receiving services in the health sciences fields; and (6) participants receiving teacher preparation services.

Training grantees may receive more than one award if the additional awards are intended to meet different absolute priorities established for the competition. ED includes an absolute priority in a grant competition to focus the competition on specific objectives or activities, and each applicant must address an absolute priority to be eligible for funding.

Research, Evaluation, and Assessments

Statutory provisions require the secretary to report annually to Congress on the performance of the TRIO programs, including performance on the outcome criteria. In addition, the secretary is expected to make grants to, or enter into contracts with, IHEs and other organizations for rigorous evaluations of effective practices of the programs. The results of such evaluations should be disseminated. Statutory provisions permit the secretary to use no more than 0.5% of the TRIO appropriation for evaluations, the peer review of applications, grantee oversight, and technical assistance. This set-aside for evaluation and other activities has contributed to a large body of TRIO evaluations.

This section will highlight recent independent evaluations, ED analyses of grantee annual performance reports (APRs), and ratings from the now out-of-use Program Assessment Rating Tool (PART). Between 2002 and 2008, the Office of Management and Budget (OMB) assessed the effectiveness of federal programs through the PART. OMB reviewed the program's purpose and design, strategic planning, management, and results/accountability. PART was expected to drive program improvement and inform federal appropriations and the legislative process. Through PART, OMB rated not performing programs as *ineffective* or *results not demonstrated* and performing programs as *adequate*, *moderately effective*, or *effective*. The results of the PART reviews are included in this report because they informed some of the HEOA amendments, which sought to improve program effectiveness.

Also in partial response to the PART, ED has published data based on APRs on program performance measures and efficiency. The data provide grantee-level results for such educational outcome measures as participant retention, enrollment, and completion. The data are expected to inform improvements in ED program management and participant educational outcomes. ED cautions against comparing results between projects since differences in incoming student characteristics are not quantified. For the same reason, APR data does not allow simple comparisons to outcomes for students who did not participate in a TRIO program.

Two issues emerge from the independent evaluations. It is difficult to establish a comparison or control group that does not limit the applicability of the findings. For instance, the comparison or control group may not have a similar risk profile to the TRIO participants, or the comparison or control group receives a treatment that is similar to that of the TRIO participants. Support services that mimic those provided by TRIO projects may supplement the TRIO services provided to TRIO participants and may be provided to the comparison or control group. Another issue is that the evaluations require many years for data collection—following students through secondary and postsecondary education, analysis, and review. For example, an SSS evaluation initiated in 1991 was published in 2010. The evaluation timeframe and legislative cycle are often not in sync.

Finally in general, the evaluation results across a series of studies indicate that the TRIO programs or similar services have a statistically significant positive effect on various academic outcome measures of subpopulation(s) of participants and, in some instances, all participants. For example, the recent SSS evaluation found that receiving supplemental services, including those from an SSS project, was associated with higher postsecondary persistence and degree completion. Also, for example, the recent Regular UB study found that the rate of postsecondary enrollment and the likelihood of earning a postsecondary credential increased significantly for the subgroup of participants who entered the program with lower educational expectations, although the program "had no detectable effect on the rate of overall postsecondary enrollment" compared to the control group.

SSS Independent Evaluations

ED contracted a six-year longitudinal evaluation of AY1991-92 freshman SSS participants and a matched comparison group. Despite efforts to select a similar comparison group, the comparison group students were less educationally and economically disadvantaged than the SSS participants. The three-year longitudinal interim evaluation, published in 1997,[42] indicated that "SSS showed a small but positive and statistically significant effect on all three measures of student outcomes," grade point averages, retention rates, and college credits earned.

An ED contractor published a study of promising practices in 1997 based on five projects identified in the aforementioned evaluation that had achieved positive, statistically significant results with respect to GPA, retention, or both.[43] The most common practices at the five exemplary sites were providing a freshman experience, emphasizing academic support for developmental and popular freshman courses, maximizing student contact, recruiting selectively, providing incentives for participation, hiring dedicated staff, and having a prominent role on campus.

---

[42] Bradford Chaney, Lana Muraskin, and Margaret Cahalan, et al., *National Study of Student Support Services: Third-Year Longitudinal Study Results and Program Implementation Study Update*, U.S. Department of Education, Washington, DC, February 1997.

[43] Lana Muraskin, *"Best Practices" in Student Support Services: A Study of Five Exemplary Sites. Followup Study of Student Support Services Program*, U.S. Department of Education, Washington, DC, August 1997.

In 2010, the contractor published the final report of the six-year longitudinal evaluation.[44] The study concluded that postsecondary supplemental services are associated with better student outcomes, generally. Participation in SSS as a freshman was associated with receiving more supplemental services from other sources as well and with a "moderate" increase in postsecondary persistence and degree completion. However, the study found that participation in SSS as a freshman was not associated with a change in the rate of transfer from two-year to four-year colleges. Receiving supplemental services from any source over the six-year period, particularly in the later years, was associated with higher postsecondary persistence and degree completion than receiving supplemental services from the SSS program during the freshman year only. Models comparing the SSS participants to students in the matched comparison group found that supplemental services were associated with a 12–19 percentage point increase in retention or degree completion, a 8–10 percentage point increase in degree attainment, and a 16 percentage point increase in transfers from two-year to four-year institutions. Models based on the number of hours of participation in various services found that supplemental services were associated with a 15–24 percentage point increase in retention or degree completion, a 11–13 percentage point increase in degree attainment, and a 10 percentage point increase in transfers from two-year to four-year institutions. The specificity of the results to SSS are limited because freshman SSS participants received supplemental services through SSS and other programs; the intensity and types of SSS services varied considerably; some individuals in the comparison group received supplemental services from non-SSS programs; and students must have persisted to receive supplemental services.

The study also found that a positive effect on student outcomes was associated with certain, specific supplemental services: home-based SSS programs, blended SSS programs, peer tutoring provided by the SSS grantee, services for disabled students provided by the SSS grantee, counseling, field trips or cultural enrichment, referrals to outside resources, services for the disabled and for those with limited English ability, college reentrance counseling, and any recent contacts with support services. Home-based SSS programs provide a home base on campus at which students may receive a broader range of services. In contrast to home-based programs, some SSS services were blended with other services on campus.

ED initiated another study of SSS promising practices in 2006. The study was scheduled for release in 2009 but is not available as of August 2012.[45]

SSS PART Reviews and Annual Performance Report Data

A 2005 OMB PART review determined that the SSS program was *moderately effective*. Moderately effective programs had ambitious goals and were well-managed but needed to improve their efficiency or address other problems in the programs' design or management in order to achieve better results. According to the review, ED had not made grantee-level performance data available publicly, had not fully met its performance goals, and had not developed targets for its program efficiency measure. An earlier 2002 OMB PART review rated

---

[44] U.S. Department of Education, Office of Planning, Evaluation and Policy Development, Policy and Program Studies Service, *National Evaluation of Student Support Services: Examination of Student Outcomes After Six Years*, Washington, DC, 2010.

[45] Office of Management and Budget, *TRIO Student Support Services Assessment*, last updated on September 6, 2008, http://georgewbush-whitehouse.archives.gov/omb/expectmore/detail/10000208.2005.html and President's Budget Request, FY2010.

the SSS program *results not demonstrated*. A rating of results not demonstrated (RND) indicated that the program had not developed acceptable performance goals or collected data to determine whether it was performing.

ED has published APR data on program performance measures and efficiency for 2005-2006 through 2009-2010.[46] Based on the 2009-2010 APRs, 74% of participants who were enrolled in the SSS project for the first-time as first-time, full-time freshmen persisted, graduated, or transferred from a two-year to a four-year IHE by the beginning of the next year. The six-year graduation rate was 42% for participants who were enrolled in the SSS project for the first-time as first-time, full-time freshmen at four-year IHEs. The three-year graduation rate was 36% for participants who were enrolled in the SSS project for the first-time as first-time, full-time freshmen at two-year IHEs.

UB Independent Evaluations

The most recent evaluation report of Regular UB was a nine-year impact study contracted by ED.[47] The study analyzed randomly assigned treatment and control groups from nationally representative projects from 1992 to 2004. The official results determined that Regular UB "had no detectable effect on the rate of overall postsecondary enrollment or the type or selectivity of postsecondary institution attended for the average eligible applicant." Postsecondary enrollment of the treatment group was 81% compared to 79% for the control group. However, the official results found that there was a five percentage-point increase in Regular UB participants earning postsecondary vocational certificates/licenses compared to nonparticipants, that the likelihood of the subgroup of Regular UB participants who entered the program with lower educational expectations earning a postsecondary degree/certificate/license increased 12 percentage-points, and that each additional year of participation in a Regular UB project resulted in a five percentage-point increase in the likelihood of receiving a bachelor's degree.

A separate analysis of the study data was completed by the ED Contracting Officer's Technical Representative[48] for the aforementioned study and published by the Council for Opportunity in Education (COE)[49] without ED endorsement. The study was intended to address a number of perceived sampling design and non-sampling error issues in the official analysis.[50] Examples of these issues included allowing one of the 67 projects sampled to represent 26% of the Regular UB

---

[46] U.S. Department of Education, " Student Support Services Program, Performance, Past Program Performance Results," http://www2.ed.gov/programs/triostudsupp/performance.html.

[47] U.S. Department of Education, Office of Planning, Evaluation and Policy Development, Policy and Program Studies Service, *The Impacts of Regular Upward Bound on Postsecondary Outcomes Seven to Nine Years After Scheduled High School Graduation*, Washington, DC, 2009.

[48] The Contracting Officer's Technical Representative (COTR) is responsible for monitoring, assessing, recording and reporting on the technical performance of the contractor on a day-to-day basis. The COTR has primary responsibility for monitoring and evaluating the contractor's work performance and deliverables. If the COTR determines that substantive changes are necessary, the COTR provides feedback to the contractor. Corrective actions based on the COTR's feedback may be initiated after negotiation between the contractor, COTR, and the contracting officer (CO) who is appointed with the authority to enter into and administer contracts on behalf of the government.

[49] COE is a nonprofit organization dedicated to furthering the expansion of college opportunities for low-income, first-generation students and students with disabilities throughout the United States. COE is the major advocacy organization for the TRIO programs.

[50] Margaret Cahalan, *Addressing Study Error in the Random Assignment National Evaluation of Upward Bound: Do the Conclusions Change?*, Council for Opportunity in Education, Washington, DC, 2009.

universe of projects and a considerable proportion of the control group population receiving services similar to those offered through the Regular UB program, including participation in a UBMS program. The alternative analysis found a 10.9 percentage-point increase in postsecondary enrollment and a 50% increase in the probability of achieving a bachelor's degree for Regular UB and UBMS participants compared to the control group. However, the alternative analysis has its own limitations. For instance, the results do not represent the Regular UB universe since a project representing 26% of the Regular UB universe was removed from consideration. Additionally, the treatment and control groups become unequally weighted because individuals were reassigned from the control to the treatment group by the analyst in instances when the individual indicated exposure to UBMS.

A component of ED's UB study evaluated a random sample of 1993-1995 UBMS participants and a comparison group of students with similar characteristics. Within four to six years of expected high school graduation, the study found that UBMS student outcomes were positive, showing an average 0.1 point GPA increase in math courses, higher enrollment in physics and chemistry courses in high school, a 10 percentage-point increase in enrollment in more selective four-year colleges, and a 6-12% increase in the completion of math and science bachelor's degrees.[51] Within seven to nine years of expected high school graduation, a second study found that participation in UBMS was associated with increased enrollment in selective four-year colleges and increased postsecondary degree completion, particularly in the social sciences.[52]

As part of the FY2007 Regular UB competition, ED included an "absolute priority" that would allow it to initiate a random assignment, control group evaluation.[53] The absolute priority set rules regarding which students would be given priority for participation in the program and called for an evaluation of the program using a control group of students who would not receive UB services. The evaluation design required all grantees to be prepared to recruit sufficient students for the control and treatment group and ensure the integrity of the control and treatment groups. Some Members of Congress and stakeholders opposed as unethical the recruiting of a control group of primarily low-income and minority students that would not receive services.[54] In addition, the selection criteria were vigorously opposed by many grantees who also questioned ED's authority, repudiated the effectiveness of recruiting a greater number of younger students, and argued that serving more students who have a high academic risk for failure would change the program's focus and effectiveness.[55] The TRIO UB "absolute priority" also required grantees to begin serving students who had completed the 8th grade, but not the 9th grade. This priority was established in response to the nine-year impact study (described earlier) that indicated that postsecondary enrollment rates increased for participants who were served multiple years.[56] The

---

[51] U.S. Department of Education, Office of Planning, Evaluation and Policy Development, Policy and Program Studies Service, *Upward Bound Math-Science: Program Description and Interim Impact Estimates*, Washington, DC, 2007.

[52] U.S. Department of Education, Office of Planning, Evaluation and Policy Development, Policy and Program Studies Service, *The Impacts of Upward Bound Math-Science on Postsecondary Outcomes 7–9 Years After Scheduled High School Graduation*, Washington, DC, 2010.

[53] The absolute priority was published by the Department of Education (ED) in the Federal Register on September 22, 2006 (71 Fed. Reg. 55447 et seq.).

[54] U.S. Congress, House Committee on Education and Labor, *College Opportunity and Affordability Act of 2007*, 110th Cong., 1st sess., December 19, 2007, H.Rept. 110-500 and Kelly Field, "Are the Right Students 'Upward Bound?,'" *The Chronicle of Higher Education*, August 17, 2007.

[55] U.S. Department of Education, "Authority to Implement a Priority in the UB Program," 71 *Federal Register* 55447, September 22, 2006.

HEOA eliminated the absolute priority for the TRIO UB program and amended the evaluation requirements to preclude excess recruiting and the denial of services as part of the evaluation methodology.

In place of ED's intended evaluation, the HEOA required a rigorous evaluation of UB identifying practices that further the achievement of a program's outcome goals to be completed by June 30, 2010. In 2010 through a contractor, ED initiated a design and feasibility study. If it is determined that a rigorous quasi-experimental evaluation of UB effective program or project practices is feasible, "A Study of Implementation and Outcomes in Upward Bound and Other TRIO Programs" may be available in 2015.[57]

ED initiated a study of UB promising practices in 2006. The study was scheduled for release in 2009 but is not available as of August 2012.[58]

UB PART Review and Annual Performance Report Data

A 2002 OMB PART review determined that the UB program was *ineffective*. According to the PART ratings, ineffective programs are not using tax dollars effectively and have been unable to achieve results due to a lack of clarity regarding the program's purpose or goals, poor management, or some other significant weakness. The review determined that UB projects do not typically target the students, those with lower expectations and at higher risk, for which the program was most effective according to an independent evaluation. The review also found that ED had not regularly conducted independent program evaluations, that program performance results were not used to manage the program, that the awarding of PE points did not encourage first-time grantees, and that the program had not achieved its performance goals.

ED has published data on Regular UB and UBMS performance measures and efficiency for 2004-2005 through 2009-2010.[59] The latest data show that the postsecondary enrollment rate of Regular UB participants expected to graduate high school in 2008-2009 was 82%, and the rate for UBMS was 90%.

In 2008, an ED contractor published an analysis of 2000-2006 academic progress data from UB and UBMS APRs matched with the students' federal financial aid files maintained by ED.[60] In

---

(...continued)

[56] U.S. Department of Education, Office of the Under Secretary, Policy and Program Studies Service, *The Impacts of Regular Upward Bound: Results from the Third Follow-Up Data Collection*, Washington, DC, 2004.

[57] U.S. Department of Education, "Notice of Submission for OMB Review," 76 *Federal Register* 22084, April 20, 2011. For more information on the study design, see Institute of Education Sciences, National Center for Education Evaluation and Regional Assistance, Evaluation Studies of the National Center for Education Evaluation and Regional Assistance, "A Study of Implementation and Outcomes in Upward Bound and Other TRIO Programs," http://ies.ed.gov/ncee/projects/evaluation/other_trio.asp.

[58] Office of Management and Budget, *TRIO Upward Bound Assessment*, last updated on September 6, 2008, http://georgewbush-whitehouse.archives.gov/omb/expectmore/detail/10000210.2002.html and President's Budget Request, FY2010.

[59] U.S. Department of Education, "Upward Bound Program, Grantee-level Performance Results," http://www2.ed.gov/programs/trioupbound/grantee-level.html.

[60] U.S. Department of Education, Office of Postsecondary Education, *Upward Bound and Upward Bound Math-Science Program Outcomes for Participants Expected to Graduate High School in 2004–05, With Supporting Data From 2005–06*, Washington, DC, 2008.

2004-2006, Regular UB grantees served seven high schools, on average, and UBMS grantees served 17, on average. Over half (59% and 55%, respectively) of participants stayed in their UB or UBMS project until their expected high school graduation date. Of participants expected to graduate in 2004-2005, 77% of UB participants and 86% of UBMS participants enrolled in postsecondary education by 2005-2006. Postsecondary enrollment increased as the length of project participation increased. For instance of participants expected to graduate in 2004-2005, 55% of one-year UB participants enrolled in postsecondary education by 2005-2006 compared to 91% of three-year or longer than three-year UB participants. For UBMS participants expected to graduate in 2004-2005, 80% of less-than-one-year participants enrolled in postsecondary education by 2005-2006 compared to 87% of one-year or longer than one-year participants. Of the participants who enrolled in postsecondary education, 45% of participants served by two-year IHE grantees enrolled at their grantee institution, 33% served by public four-year IHE grantees enrolled at their grantee institution, and 11% served by private four-year IHE grantees enrolled at their grantee institution.

TS Evaluations

In 2004, an ED contractor released the *Final Report from Phase I of the National Evaluation*.[61] The report primarily described the program's history, grant recipients, program staff, program activities, and program participants through 1999. The evaluation also compared project outcomes to the goals established by the individual projects. In 1998-1999, the majority (87%) of projects achieved their secondary school graduation goal; 53% achieved their postsecondary admissions goal; and 38% achieved their postsecondary re-entry goal. On average, 71% of high school graduates enrolled in postsecondary education compared to the average goal of 75%.

Phase II of the National Evaluation culminated in a limited quasi-experimental study of 1995-96 ninth graders in Florida, Indiana, and Texas.[62] The study, released in 2006, found that TS participants applied for financial aid at rates 17, 14, and 28 percentage points higher than nonparticipant comparison students in Florida, Indiana, and Texas, respectively. The study also found that the rate of enrollment of TS participants in public colleges and universities was 14, 6, and 18 percentage points higher for Florida, Indiana, and Texas, respectively, than for the nonparticipant comparison groups. Postsecondary enrollment data was only available for public colleges in the states of Florida, Indiana, and Texas.

TS PART Review and Annual Performance Report Data

A 2005 OMB PART review determined that the TS program was *moderately effective*. The review determined that ED still needed to make grantee-level performance data available publicly, meet all of its program performance goals, and develop targets for its program efficiency measure.

---

[61] U.S. Department of Education, Office of the Under Secretary, Policy and Program Studies Service, *Implementation of the Talent Search Program, Past and Present, Final Report from Phase I of the National Evaluation*, Washington, DC, 2004, http://www2.ed.gov/rschstat/eval/highered/talentsearch/talentreport.pdf.

[62] U.S. Department of Education, Office of Planning, Evaluation and Policy Development, Policy and Program Studies Service, *A Study of the Effect of the Talent Search Program on Secondary and Postsecondary Outcomes in Florida, Indiana and Texas: Final Report From Phase II of the National Evaluation*, Washington, DC, 2006.

ED has published data on program performance measures and efficiency for 2006-2007 through 2009-2010.[63] According to the 2009-2010 data, 80% of college-ready participants enrolled in postsecondary education and 89% applied for financial aid. College-ready participants are high school seniors or the equivalent, high school graduates that have not enrolled in postsecondary education or the equivalent, postsecondary dropouts, and potential postsecondary transfers. The enrollment rate of college-ready participants was higher (83%) for participants not served by IHEs than for participants served by two-year IHE grantees (78%) and participants served by four-year IHEs (80%). Also, participants were more likely to enroll in a college of the same level (two-year or four-year) as sponsored the TS program. For example, 57% of participants served by two-year IHEs enrolled in two-year IHEs compared to the 60% of participants served by four-year IHEs that enrolled in four-year IHEs.

EOC Evaluations

The evaluation of TS in 2004 included an appendix describing EOC history, grant recipients, program staff, program activities, and program participants based on a 1999-2000 survey of project directors and 1998-99 annual performance reports. Little data on student outcomes was available. Of the 16% of EOC projects that reported a goal for secondary school completion, the average goal was 58%, and the average completion rate was 93%. Of the 79% of EOC projects that reported a goal for postsecondary admissions, the average goal was 49%, and the average admissions rate was 51%. Finally of the 67% of EOC projects that reported a goal for postsecondary re-entry, the average goal was 46%, and the average re-entry rate was 56%.

CRS has not been able to identify any rigorous evaluations of EOC as of the date of this report.

EOC PART Review and Annual Performance Report Data

A 2007 OMB PART review rated the EOC program *results not demonstrated*. The program scored indefinitively because ED had not conducted a recent independent evaluation, had no baseline or targets for measuring and achieving efficiencies and cost effectiveness in program execution, had yet to analyze grantee level performance, and failed to meet some of its annual performance goals.

ED has published data on program performance measures and efficiency for 2006-2007 through 2009-2010.[64] According to the 2009-2010 data, 60% of college-ready participants enrolled in postsecondary education. College-ready participants are high school seniors or their equivalent, high school graduates that have not enrolled in postsecondary education or their equivalent, postsecondary dropouts, and potential postsecondary transfers. The enrollment rate of college-ready participants was higher (62%) for participants served by two-year IHE grantees than for participants served by four-year IHEs (59%) or other organizations (61%). As in the TS program, participants were more likely to enroll in a college of the same level (two-year or four-year) as sponsored the EOC program. Specifically, 79% of participants served by two-year IHEs enrolled

---

[63] U.S. Department of Education, "Talent Search Program, Grantee-level Performance Results," http://www2.ed.gov/programs/triotalent/grantee-level.html.

[64] U.S. Department of Education, "Grantee-level Performance Results," http://www2.ed.gov/programs/trioeoc/grantee-level.html.

in two-year IHEs compared to the 53% of participants served by four-year IHEs that enrolled in two-year IHEs.

McNair Independent Evaluations

In 2008, an ED contractor released a report of educational and employment outcomes based on a descriptive analysis of prior McNair participants.[65] The report found that 73% of McNair participants enrolled in graduate school within five to seven years of completing a bachelor's degree, compared to 30% of all bachelor's degree recipients. The report also found that 44% of McNair participants earned a master's degree, 14.4% earned a doctorate degree, and 12.1% earned a professional degree within 10 years of program participation. It is important to note that the findings presented in the report were not the result of a random assignment study design and that there may be differences in the propensity to enroll in graduate school between McNair participants and all bachelor's degree recipients.

McNair PART Review and Annual Performance Report Data

A 2006 OMB PART review determined that the McNair program was *moderately effective*. The program was in the early stages of measuring and achieving efficiencies and cost effectiveness in program execution, and the program had not made grantee-level performance data available publicly.

ED has published data on a program performance measure for 2005-2006 through 2009-2010.[66] On average, 70% of McNair participants who received their bachelor's degree in 2006-2007 enrolled in graduate school within three years.

Training Evaluations

A major evaluation of the program has not been conducted, and ED does not publish grantee-level performance results.

Author Contact Information

Cassandria Dortch
Analyst in Education Policy
cdortch@crs.loc.gov, 7-0376

---

[65] U.S. Department of Education, Office of Planning, Evaluation and Policy Development, Policy and Program Studies Service, *Education and Employment Outcomes of the Ronald E. McNair Postbaccalaureate Achievement Program Alumni*, Washington, DC, 2008.

[66] U.S. Department of Education, "Ronald E. McNair Postbaccalaureate Achievement Program, Performance, Grantee-level Performance Results," http://www2.ed.gov/programs/triomcnair/performance.html.

www.ingramcontent.com/pod-product-compliance
Lightning Source LLC
Chambersburg PA
CBHW081245180526
45171CB00005B/546